Philadelphia's Best Buildings

In [and Near] Center City

Prepared for the Foundation for Architecture
by the Group for Environmental Education, Inc.
John Andrew Gallery, Project Director

Published by the Foundation for Architecture
Philadelphia, Pennsylvania 19103

COPYRIGHT © 1994 BY THE FOUNDATION FOR ARCHITECTURE

ALL RIGHTS RESERVED. NO PART OF THIS BOOK MAY BE REPRODUCED IN ANY
FORMS BY ANY ELECTRONIC OR MECHANICAL MEANS (INCLUDING PHOTOCOPYING,
RECORDING, OR INFORMATION STORAGE AND RETRIEVAL) WITHOUT PERMISSION IN
WRITING FROM THE PUBLISHER.

LIBRARY OF CONGRESS CATALOG CARD NUMBER: 94-072346

ISBN 0-9622908-2-3 (PBK.)

PRINTED AND BOUND IN THE UNITED STATES

DESIGN BY JOEL KATZ DESIGN ASSOCIATES
PHOTOGRAPHS COPYRIGHT ©1994 BY PETER B. OLSON
PRINTED BY STRINE PRINTING CO

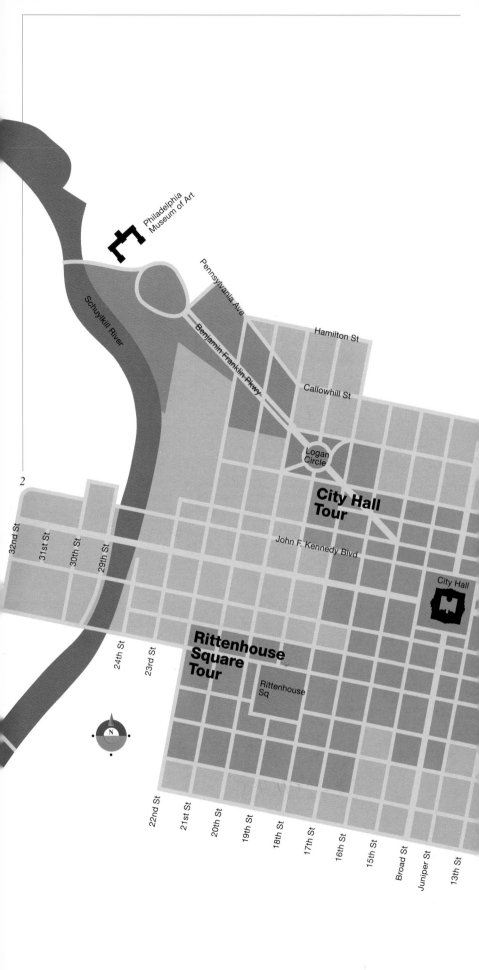

Philadelphia Museum of Art

Schuylkill River

Pennsylvania Ave

Benjamin Franklin Pkwy

Hamilton St

Callowhill St

Logan Circle

City Hall Tour

John F. Kennedy Blvd

City Hall

Rittenhouse Square Tour

Rittenhouse Sq

32nd St
31st St
30th St
29th St
24th St
23rd St
22nd St
21st St
20th St
19th St
18th St
17th St
16th St
15th St
Broad St
Juniper St
13th St

N

Contents

Introduction

Philadelphia, more than any other American city, represents the history of architecture in the United States. Throughout the city are outstanding examples of every important architectural style and architectural period in the country's history. Most visitors to Philadelphia do not have the time to see this vast wealth of resources. For those who do, the companion volume to this book, *Philadelphia Architecture: A Guide to the City*, describes and illustrates 253 buildings and contains eight walking tours and a driving tour.

But everyone sees important buildings while visiting historic and cultural institutions or while walking from hotels to restaurants, museums or the Convention Center. This book is intended for visitors and residents who have limited time, but would like to know which of Philadelphia's best buildings can be seen easily in and near Center City.

Most of the best buildings in Center City are concentrated in four areas: Old City and Society Hill, the center of colonial Philadelphia; the Rittenhouse Square area, an important 19th century neighborhood; and the City Hall area, the location of the important civic and commercial buildings. The first four sections of the book are walking tours of these areas. The best buildings in each area are indicated by numbers preceding the building name in the text, with corresponding numbers on the tour maps. Each of these buildings is illustrated and described. Other noteworthy buildings along the tour route are indicated by letters and briefly described.

The four walking tours are followed by descriptions and illustrations of other important buildings in Center City and the best buildings near Center City that can be reached easily by subway, bus or taxi. One building outside the city is included because it is the only major work by Frank Lloyd Wright in the Philadelphia area.

Center City Philadelphia

The plan of Center City Philadelphia was created by William Penn and his surveyor, Thomas Holme. Originally, the city occupied the area between the Delaware and Schuylkill rivers, bounded by Vine Street on the north and South Street on the south. The plan of the city was a grid of streets, with greater emphasis on the center east/west street (Market) and the center north/south street (Broad). These two streets intersected in a central square designated by Penn for civic buildings. Center Square was once the location of a Quaker meeting house and later the city's first water works before City Hall was built there in 1894.

The grid of streets was interrupted by four other squares, one in each quadrant of the city. These were intended as public parks in the center of residential areas. All four squares remain today. Washington and Rittenhouse Squares are closest to the original concept of generous parks surrounded by fine neighborhoods. Franklin Square has been compromised by an adjacent expressway and Logan Square was transformed into a very handsome civic square with a magnificent fountain by Alexander Sterling Calder at the time of the construction of the Benjamin Franklin Parkway in 1917–24.

The original settlement of the city was along the Delaware River bank, generally in the area from Chestnut to Vine streets, Front to 5th streets. This area is now known as Old City. But expansion to the south, into what is now known as

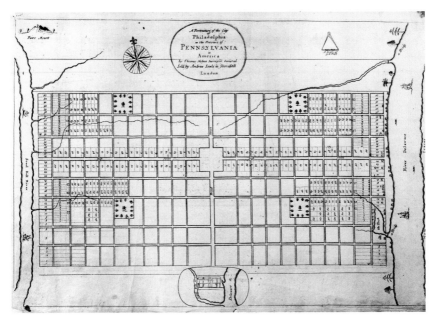

Thomas Holme's plan
of the City of
Philadelphia, 1682

Society Hill, began very early. These two areas contain the earliest houses, churches and institutional buildings. As the city grew in the 18th and 19th centuries, residential development expanded westward from Society Hill to the Schuylkill River. At the same time, commercial development expanded westward along and north of Market Street, accompanied by the development of railroad stations and the placement of City Hall on Center Square.

But Philadelphia's growth was not confined to this area defined by Penn as the original city. Outside these early boundaries other settlements began north and south of Center City, west of the Schuylkill River and in Germantown and Chestnut Hill to the northwest. By 1854, settlement of this surrounding region was so extensive, the legal boundaries of the city were consolidated with the boundaries of the county, creating the legal limits of Philadelphia as we know it today.

The four tours follow this pattern of growth. The first covers Old City, the earliest residential area but now an area dominated by later commercial buildings. The second tour covers Society Hill, an important colonial neighborhood and the location of more authentic 18th century buildings than any other place in the country. The third tour is of the Rittenhouse Square area, one of the city's finest 19th century residential neighborhoods. The final tour covers the area around City Hall and includes many important civic and institutional buildings as well as the city's most important office buildings.

5

Old City Tour

Old City was the first residential area in Philadelphia and contained the city's earliest houses, religious and civic buildings. In the 18th century, the city's principal markets were located along Market Street from Front to 3rd streets. These activities encouraged commercial development in the blocks immediately north and south. By the end of the 19th century, most of the houses had been displaced by commercial buildings. Now the area is noteworthy for its fine examples of 18th and 19th century commercial architecture of different styles and materials ranging from brick, terra cotta and marble to cast iron. Many of the buildings have been converted to apartments as Old City has once again become a desirable residential neighborhood.

To reach the start of the Old City tour, take a bus on Market or Chestnut streets or the Market-Frankford subway line to 2nd Street.

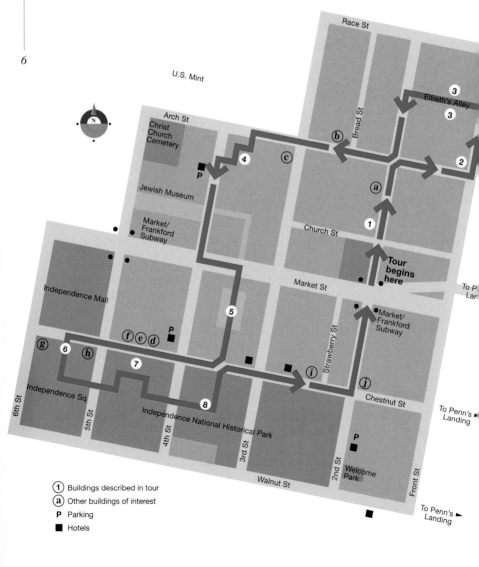

The tour begins at 2nd and Market streets and proceeds north and west past important colonial buildings and distinctive examples of 19th century commercial architecture.

The first building on the tour is **(1) Christ Church** (1727–44), 2nd and Market streets.

Although Penn founded Philadelphia to provide a refuge for Quakers, he extended freedom of worship to all religions. One of the first groups to exercise this right was the Anglicans of the Church of England. They modeled their new church on the work of Sir Christopher Wren, the English architect who rebuilt fifty-two churches in London after the Great Fire. Construction was supervised by John Kearsley, a physician, who probably was responsible for the design. He was the first of many gentlemen-architects who designed important civic buildings.

Christ Church is symmetrical in plan and elevation. The decoration on the facade is classical. Two-story brick pilasters alternate rhythmically with round arch windows. The cornice is decorated with medallions, and a balustrade hides the vertical slope of the roof. On the east end, a large Palladian window provides light for the chancel. The classical forms are made more dramatic by the strong curving lines of fat scrolls on the east pediment and by the robust curves of the roof urns, capped by carved flames.

Christ Church
1727-44
Dr. John Kearsley,
supervisor
Open to the public

Christ Church was the most sumptuous building in the colonies and the most sophisticated example of Georgian design. Robert Smith, the most prominent master carpenter of the time, worked on the steeple, which was added in 1751–54. It was also designed with classical details: round arch windows, pilasters and pediments over circular windows. The brick tower was finished quickly, but it took three lotteries, sponsored by Benjamin Franklin, to raise enough money to add the wooden part. The 196-foot steeple, probably the tallest in the colonies, was a prominent landmark on the early Philadelphia skyline.

From Christ Church walk north on 2nd Street. About halfway up the block on the west side of the street is the **(a) Tutlemann Brothers and Faggen Building** (1830–36/ 1900–01), 56–60 North 2nd Street. It is one of the many commercial buildings that have been converted to apartments. The cast-iron facade may have been the last erected in this country.

At Arch Street turn right and proceed to the end of the block. On the north side is the **(2) Smythe Buildings** (1855–57), 101–111 Arch Street.

The introduction of cast-iron facades made it possible to achieve the architectural effects of the Italianate style—popular for 19th century residential design—on commercial buildings in an economical manner. The facade of the Smythe Buildings is the best example of cast-iron design remaining in Philadelphia. The facade was produced by the Tiffany and Bottom Foundry in Trenton, New Jersey and probably designed by a company draftsman. The building originally extended half a block with a continuous facade composed of the delicate cast-iron columns and arched windows. In addition to its rich appearance at relatively low cost, cast iron appealed to the

Smythe Buildings
1855–57

7

commercial developer because of the ease of construction and the large amount of window area relative to the structural support required for the facade.

The central bay of the Smythe Buildings was demolished in 1913 to make way for a trolley turn-around. When the building was converted to apartments in 1986 (Hans P. Stein Architects), it was reconstructed in fiber glass from old section molds so carefully that it is difficult to detect the difference.

Turn left at the corner onto Front Street and walk north to **(3) Elfreth's Alley,** *then turn left.*

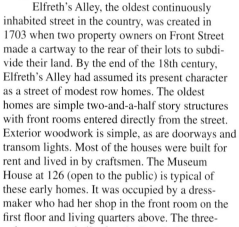

Elfreth's Alley, the oldest continuously inhabited street in the country, was created in 1703 when two property owners on Front Street made a cartway to the rear of their lots to subdivide their land. By the end of the 18th century, Elfreth's Alley had assumed its present character as a street of modest row homes. The oldest homes are simple two-and-a-half story structures with front rooms entered directly from the street. Exterior woodwork is simple, as are doorways and transom lights. Most of the houses were built for rent and lived in by craftsmen. The Museum House at 126 (open to the public) is typical of these early homes. It was occupied by a dressmaker who had her shop in the front room on the first floor and living quarters above. The three-and-a-half-story houses were built after the Revolutionary War and show the influence of the Federal style in the classically framed doorways with pilasters and pediments.

Elfreth's Alley
from 1720
Private residences

8

The walk down Elfreth's Alley ends at 2nd Street. Turn left to Arch Street and then turn right and proceed past 3rd Street.
Along the way you will pass the **(b) Betsy Ross House** (1740), 239 Arch Street, which is similar in character, scale and design to the older houses on Elfreth's Alley.

At the southwest corner of 3rd and Arch streets is the **(c) St. Charles Hotel** (1851), 60–66 North 3rd Street, Charles Rubican, builder. The facade is actually cast iron but it was painted with sand added to the paint to create the color and texture of stone. It was converted to apartments in 1980 (Adaptive Design, architects).

Just past 3rd Street on the left is the **(4) Arch Street Friends Meeting House** (1803–05/ 1810–11), 330 Arch Street.

William Penn and many of the original settlers of Philadelphia were members of the Religious Society of Friends, commonly known as Quakers. Friends worshiped in gatherings without a minister and shared their spiritual

Arch Street Friends Meeting House
1803–05/1810–11
Owen Biddle
Open to the public

thoughts. The meeting houses built for their services usually contained two rooms: a large entrance and gathering room and the meeting room itself.

The Arch Street Meeting House is the largest in the city and second oldest. There are two rooms in the central structure and two flanking wings used for annual meetings, when men and women met separately.

The building is a plain brick structure with flat exterior surfaces, marble steps, wood shutters and simple columned porticos over the doors. The center structure and east wing were designed by Owen Biddle author of the influential trade book, Young Carpenter's Assistant (1805).

After visiting the Meeting House, walk through the grounds and exit by the west gate to 3rd Street, then turn left. After crossing Market Street, turn left again to the middle of the block to **(5) Franklin Court,** 312–22 Market Street.

Franklin Court
restored 1973–76
Venturi and Rauch,
with John Milner
Associates
Open to the public

Benjamin Franklin built his own house and print shop in the courtyard behind a row of tenant buildings on Market Street. Although the tenant buildings survived, Franklin's house, except for sections of foundations, was destroyed. Lacking sufficient evidence to reconstruct the house faithfully, the National Park Service commissioned the architects to design an interpretive complex.

The complex consists of four elements: the Market Street buildings, a garden, the "ghost structure" representing the house and print shop, and an underground museum. The most original aspect of the design is the white tubular-steel frames outlining Franklin's original buildings. The plans of the house and print shop are inlaid in the paving beneath the frames, supplemented by quotes from Franklin and his wife cut into the slate paving. Beneath the ghost structure and 18th century garden is a museum, reached by a long, sloping ramp. The museum contains imaginative exhibits about Franklin's life and accomplishments including banks of telephones from which you can call important historical figures and hear their views on Franklin. The restored Market Street buildings also interpret Franklin's activities; one contains a post office and another a print shop.

Leave Franklin Court by the Chestnut Street exit then turn right and proceed along Chestnut to 5th Street. This portion of Chestnut Street was the city's financial district in the 19th century. Many of the original bank buildings have been demolished and those that remain have been converted to other uses. The most noteworthy remaining buildings are the **(d) Bank of Pennsylvania** (1857–59), 421 Chestnut Street, John M. Gries, architect; **(e) the Farmers' and Mechanics' Bank** (1854–55), 427 Chestnut Street, John M. Gries, architect; and **(f) the Pennsylvania Company for Insurances on Lives and Granting Annuities** (1871–73), 431 Chestnut Street, Addison Hutton, architect.

Between 5th and 6th streets along Chestnut Street is the **(6) Independence Hall complex** and the entrance to Independence National Historical Park.

In 1729, Philadelphia lawmakers decided to move the government from the cramped quarters of the Town Hall at 2nd and Market streets to a site at Chestnut Street between 5th and 6th streets even though it was on the outskirts of town. The State House, as it was originally known, is an outstanding example of Georgian design. Although it was an important civic building, it is not as elaborate as Christ Church and, in fact, is domestic in scale and detail. The main building is a self-contained rectangular block, visually framed by quoins or corner stones. The cornice, balustrade, belt courses and water table emphasize the horizontal and contribute to the feeling of domestic scale. The

9

6

**Independence Hall
(State House)**
1732–48
Alexander Hamilton
with Edmund Wooley
Open to the public

10

soapstone panels between the second and first floors, the marble keystones and acanthus-carved medallions provide restrained decoration for the facade.

In 1750, the Assembly voted to commemorate the fifty years of Penn's Charter of Liberties by adding a tower to the rear of the State House. At the same time, a large clock was built against the west end of the building. The long case, made of rusticated stone, hid the weights and lines necessary for an eight-day clock.

The turbulent years before the Revolutionary War were the high point in the history of the State House. The Assembly Room, the setting for dramatic debates on independence, was the room in which the Declaration of Independence was signed. For ten years (1790–1800), the State House was the capital of the new nation before the government moved to Washington.

In 1830, John Haviland, the Greek Revival architect, was hired by the city to restore the building to attract new tenants. His restoration marked the first of many. In 1950, the National Park Service undertook an archeological study of State House buildings, which provided the information necessary to restore them to their 1776 appearance.

The two buildings flanking Independence Hall are **(g) Congress Hall** (1787–89) and the **(h) U.S. Supreme Court** (1790–91). Although planned as early as 1736, these two buildings were not built until after the Revolutionary War when the Federal style was more popular. The difference is evident in the more delicate treatment of window mullions and cornice detailing.

The National Park Service gives tours of the Independence Hall complex and all other buildings in the park.

Walk through Independence Square behind Independence Hall and cross 5th Street to the cobbled street in the center of the block. In the middle of the block is the **(7) Second Bank of the United States** (1818–24).

The Second Bank was founded in 1816. When the bank held a competition for the design of its new building, Nicholas Biddle, president of the bank, required all architects to use the Greek style. Strickland's design is one of the first Greek Revival public buildings in the country. Modeled on the Parthenon in Athens, it features plain Doric columns and little decoration. The structure appears to be solid marble, but really is brick faced with marble. In contrast to the Greek exterior, the interior is Roman. A barrel-vaulted ceiling covers the banking hall.

The building is now the National Portrait Gallery, containing many of Charles Wilson Peale's portraits of the nation's founders.

7

**Second Bank of the
United States**
1818–24
William Strickland
Open to the public

Carpenters' Hall
1770–74
Robert Smith
Open to the public

Continue to walk east, crossing 4th Street. Directly ahead is **(8) Carpenters' Hall** (1770–74).

In the 18th century, building trades in the city were dominated by members of the Carpenters' Company. The company was founded in 1724 and modeled after English builders' guilds. In addition to building design and construction, members assisted contractors and clients in determining the fair value of completed work.

Robert Smith, a member, was chosen to design the company's meeting place. He created a cruciform plan based on one of Palladio's Italian villas and the town halls of his native Scotland. The building's details are Georgian, such as the pediments over the north and south doors and the cupola on the roof. The first floor was a large meeting hall; the second was divided into smaller meeting rooms. The members used the hall for their meetings, but also rented space to other organizations. The most famous group to use the hall was the Continental Congress in 1774.

At this point it is possible to continue on to the Society Hill tour (page 12) or return to Chestnut Street and walk east to 2nd Street, then turn left and return to 2nd and Market streets where this tour began. Along this return route are the **(i) Leland and Elliot Buildings** (1854–56), 235–37 Chestnut Street, Joseph C. Hoxie, architect and the **(j) Corn Exchange** (1900–01), 2nd and Chestnut streets, Newman, Woodman and Harris, architects. The Leland and Elliot buildings are fine examples of the Italianate commercial style popular in the 19th century. The five story high granite facades express the structural system and allow large windows. The Corn Exchange was established to serve merchants trading in grain and groceries. The brick building is based on the Georgian style but enriched with elaborate Baroque stone carvings.

11

Society Hill Tour

Society Hill contains the largest concentration of original 18th century architecture of any place in the United States. As one of the principal residential areas of colonial Philadelphia, the neighborhood included homes of the wealthy and poor, prominent churches, markets and taverns.

When the population of the city moved westward in the 19th century, Society Hill deteriorated and became an area of dilapidated houses and commercial buildings dominated by the city's wholesale food market. Today, as a result of a major urban renewal program begun in the 1950s by the city, state and federal governments, it is one of the most attractive and affluent neighborhoods in Philadelphia. All the 18th century buildings in the area have been restored, and parks and landscaped walkways created to replace demolished buildings. Where sites were available for new construction, the best modern design was encouraged to contrast with the original colonial buildings. The neighborhood was named Society Hill after the 18th-century Society of Free Traders which had its offices on the hill above Dock Creek.

The easiest way to reach Society Hill tour is to take a Market or Chestnut street bus or the Market-Frankford subway line to 5th Street.

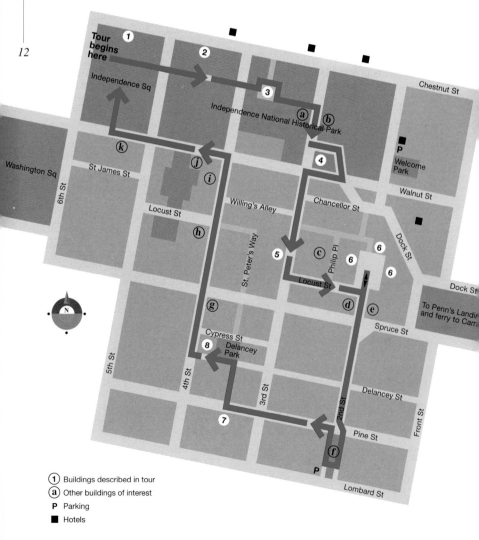

(1) Buildings described in tour
(a) Other buildings of interest
P Parking
■ Hotels

The tour begins at Independence Square, proceeds through the National Park and then through Society Hill, returning to Independence Square.

The first three buildings on the tour—**(1) Independence Hall, (2) the Second Bank of the United States** and **(3) Carpenters' Hall**—are also the last three buildings on the Old City tour. All three are located along Chestnut Street between 5th and 6th streets. See pages 9–11 for descriptions of these buildings.

After leaving Carpenters' Hall, continue east to 3rd Street, then turn right and walk past the **(a) First Bank of the United States** (1795–97/1901), 120 South 3rd Street, Samuel Blodgett and James Windrim, architects. This was the first national bank in the country, created by Alexander Hamilton, and the most imposing structure of its day. Across the street is the **(b) Independence National Park Visitors Center** (1976), 125 South 3rd Street, Cambridge Seven Associates.

Just past the Visitors Center is the **(4) Merchants' Exchange** (1832–33), 143 South 3rd Street.

4

When Philadelphia businesses became too numerous to meet in coffee houses and taverns, merchants formed the Philadelphia Exchange Company. Strickland designed their building, now the oldest stock exchange in the country, which was considered to be one of the most beautiful structures of its kind.

The building consists of a rectangular main structure with a semi-circular portico. Strickland used the Corinthian order on the colonnade, reflecting the evolution of a more elaborate Greek Revival style from his earlier design for the Second Bank of the United States on Chestnut Street. He crowned the building with a lantern meticulously copied from the Choragic Monument of Lysicrates, one of the most copied ancient Greek monuments of the period.

**Merchants'
Exchange**
1832–33
William Strickland

The Exchange Room, in the curved portion of the building, was sumptuous. It had a mosaic floor, a domed ceiling supported on marble columns and frescoes on the walls. The Exchange dissolved during the Civil War. When wholesale food markets took over the area, sheds were erected around the east end of the building. These remained until 1952, when the Exchange was purchased by the National Park Service and adapted for its offices.

After walking around the Merchants' Exchange, proceed south on 3rd Street, passing from the National Park into the Society Hill residential neighborhood. On the right is the **(5) Powel House** (1765), 244 South 3rd Street.

5

The Powel House is the finest Georgian row house in the city. It was built by Charles Stedman. Before he could live in it, he sold it to Samuel Powel, the first mayor of Philadelphia after the revolution. Powel was a Quaker who later turned Anglican. This change can be seen in his house. The restrained exterior reflects the Quaker concern for simplicity. The brick facade is Flemish bond, with cheaper common bond on the side. The only decoration is the Doric frame surrounding the door. Inside, restraint gives way to luxurious rooms decorated with fine paneling, elaborate carving and delicate plaster work.

Powel House
1765
Open to the public

13

The plan of the house is quite sophisticated compared to the typical town house. The front door enters into a generous hall. The parlor and dining rooms are to one side, and at the rear, framed by a large arch, is an open mahogany staircase. A ballroom with elaborate woodwork and plaster ceiling is on the second floor. Robert Smith, the prominent carpenter-architect, worked on this interior.

Cross 3rd Street to the east side and then proceed east on Locust Walk to the (c) **Society Hill Townhouses** (1962) *and the* **(6) Society Hill Towers** (1964), 200 Locust Street.

When the city decided to redevelop the Society Hill area in the 1950's, the wholesale food markets were relocated to a new food distribution center, and a competition held to select a housing design that would symbolize the renewal of the area. I. M. Pei's winning entry included the townhouses on 3rd Street and the three tall apartment buildings located on the axis of 2nd Street.

The townhouses, built in 1962, provide a transition between the towers and the 18th and 19th century row houses on 3rd Street. The three story houses with dark brick facades are clustered around a landscaped parking court containing the sculpture *Floating Figure* by Gaston Lachaise. The towers are constructed of poured-in-place concrete, divided into meticulous rectilinear units that are both the structural frame and the facade. Each apartment has floor-to-ceiling glass windows, which provide dramatic views of the river and the city. The entrance court contains the sculptural group *Old Man, Young Man, The Future* by Leonard Baskin.

Society Hill Towers
1964
I.M. Pei and
Associates
Private residences

14

From the Towers, walk south on 2nd Street past the (d) **Abercrombie House** (1759), 268–70 South 2nd Street, a fine example of Georgian residential design, and the (e) **Man Full of Trouble Tavern** (1760), 127 Spruce Street. In colonial times, taverns were places for socializing. This one had rooms for travelers on the second floor and in the attic, whose gambrel roof gave more room than the common pitched roof.

Continue south on 2nd Street to Pine Street and the (f) **Head House and Market Shed** (1745/1804) which was the city's second market. These are the oldest buildings of their kind in the country. The shed provided stalls for farmers to set up carts and, by 1777, extended to South Street. The Head House at Pine Street was added in 1804. It housed fire apparatus and served as a meeting place for volunteer fire companies.

After walking around the Market Shed return to Pine Street and turn left, proceeding along Pine past 3rd Street to **(7) St. Peter's Church** (1758–61).

By 1750, Christ Church at 2nd and Market streets could no longer accommodate the number of people who wanted to have seats there. It also was inconvenient for parishioners living south of Walnut Street. The Penn family donated land for a second Anglican church, the "chapel of ease" as St. Peter's was first called. Robert Smith designed and built the church. Dr. John Kearsley, who had directed work on Christ Church was the supervisor.

St. Peter's is a subdued version of a Palladian church. It contains a grand Palladian window on the chancel wall, and the

St. Peter's Church
1758–61
Robert Smith,
carpenter-architect
Open to the public

sides of the church are pierced by round arch windows, but there is an absence of elaborate detail. St. Peter's still retains its original high-backed pews, raised off the floor to keep out drafts. In an unusual arrangement, the altar and pulpit are at opposite ends of the main aisle.

The steeple was added in 1852 by William Strickland. The simple tower, six stories high, is in keeping with the church's restrained exterior.

Across from St. Peter's is one of the many landscaped walkways that pass through Society Hill. *Take the walkway to Delancey Street, turn left and at the corner of 4th and Delancey streets is the* **(8) Hill-Physick-Keith House** (1786), 321 South 4th Street.

8

This house is the only remaining example of the many freestanding mansions that once existed within the rowhouse fabric of the colonial city. It is also one of the finest examples of Federal-style architecture. Colonel Henry Hill, a prosperous wine merchant, built the house, which was later owned by Dr. Philip Syng Physick, the father of American surgery.

Federal-style ornamentation is more delicate than its Georgian predecessor. On the Hill-Physick-Keith House, ornament is limited to projecting keystones and cornice medallions. Brick courses, separating the floors and outlining the main door, are nearly flush with the wall surface. The finely crafted double door, surrounded by intricate carving and topped by an impressive fanlight, imparts a grace and monumentality more often found on country mansions. The spacious interior contains thirty-two rooms, including a ballroom on the first floor finished with elaborate woodwork.

Hill-Physick-Keith House
1786
Open to the Public

15

Leaving the Hill-Physick-Keith House, walk north on 4th Street to Walnut Street. Along the way are several noteworthy buildings. Near the corner of 4th and Spruce streets is **(g) Girard Row** *(*1831–32*)*, 326–34 Spruce Street, a handsome group of houses designed by William Struthers for Stephen Girard, millionaire banker and merchant. Farther along 4th Street is the **(h) Shippen-Wistar House** (1765) 238 South 4th Street. The **(i) Philadelphia Contributionship for Insuring of Houses from Loss by Fire** (1835–36), 212 South 4th Street, was designed by Thomas U. Walter. The Contributionship, founded by Benjamin Franklin, is the oldest mutual fire insurance company in the country. Its building is a simple brick structure with an elegant portico supported by fluted marble Corinthian columns.

At 4th and Walnut streets, turn left and proceed past 5th Street to the center of the block to return to Independence Square. The **(j) Center for Judaic Studies** (1992), 425 Walnut Street, Geddes Brecher Qualls Cunningham, architects, is an fine example of contemporary design that respects the traditions of the colonial period. Also take note of the distinctive **(k) Penn Mutual Life Insurance Co. Addition** (1969–70), Mitchell/Giurgola Associates, architects, 510 Walnut Street. The design incorporates the 1838 Egyptian Revival facade of John Haviland's Pennsylvania Fire insurance Company.

The tour ends at Independence Square.

Rittenhouse Square Tour

Rittenhouse Square is one of the original public places set aside in Penn's plan for the city. Up until the 1850's development of the city remained east of Broad Street. However, at that time many wealthy families decided to skip over the vacant land west of Broad Street to build elegant mansions around Rittenhouse Square. This encouraged speculative developers to follow and build large Victorian row houses, which in turn were followed by the construction of large churches.

The residential area around the square continues to be one of the city's finest neighborhoods and contains exceptional examples of 19th century row houses, including many of the best brownstones in the city. Rittenhouse Square itself is an important meeting place and the scene of outdoor art exhibits, concerts and a wide variety of public events.

The easiest way to reach the Rittenhouse Square area is to take a bus on Walnut or Chestnut streets and walk south on 18th Street.

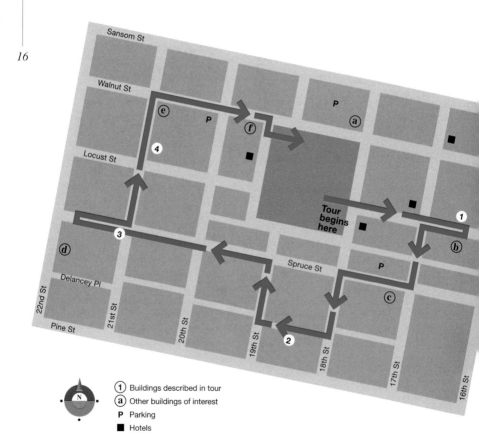

The tour begins in Rittenhouse Square. Few large mansions remain around the square, but the **(a) Fell-Van Rensselaer House** (1896–98), 1801–03 Walnut Street, by Peabody and Stearns, gives a sense of the scale and character of mansions of the period. Leave the square and proceed east along Locust Street past 17th Street to **(1) St. Mark's Church** (1848–51), 1625 Locust Street.

The founders of St. Mark's were influenced by the Anglican reform movement, which advocated correct medieval Gothic design as a way of returning spiritual ardor to the church. The exterior of the church is in keeping with the 19th-century interest in picturesque design. Each of the elements is given separate expression, in contrast to the simple rectangular form of 18th-century churches. The tower and entrance door are set off from the nave, the center aisle and side aisles are expressed by different rooflines, and the chancel is a separate mass with a lower roofline.

As was typical of medieval churches, construction materials are left in their natural condition on the interior. This gives the church an unusually impressive character. The walls and ceiling are of hammer-dressed stone, and the exposed trusses are of oak. Gothic details are present in the pointed arch windows with tracery, the quatrefoil shapes of the piers and on the capitals of the piers, some of which were left uncarved to symbolize that the work of the church is never finished.

St. Mark's Church
1848–51
John Notman
Open to the public

The church has been enriched by gifts of the faithful, of which the most impressive are the Lady Chapel, designed by Cope and Stewardson from 1899–1902, and the richly sculpted silver altar, both donated by Rodman Wanamaker.

This block **(b)** of **Locust Street** also contains a number of elegant houses designed by prominent 19th and early 20th century architects. Italian Renaissance Revival brownstones predominate on the south side of the block. Numbers 1604, 1620, and 1622 have ben attributed to John Notman. The brownstone at 1618 was altered at the turn of the century by Wilson Eyre. The frame of the first-floor window is carved in rich floral motifs with a human face emerging from the swirling leaves. The two houses at 1631–33 Locust St. by Cope and Stewardson reflect the late 19th-century taste for Georgian Revival. The white limestone Beaux-Arts style house at 1629 was designed by Horace Trumbauer. Frank Miles Day designed the house at 235 South 17th Street in a medieval style with gables, bay windows and dark brick offset by limestone trim.

17

Return to 17th Street and turn left to Spruce Street. The **(c) Tenth Presbyterian Church** (1854), 1700 Spruce Street, was designed by John McArthur, Jr., architect of City Hall. *Turn right on Spruce Street and proceed to 18th Street. At 18th Street go left half a block and turn right onto the 1800 Block of* **(2) Delancey Place** (1853–80).

1800 Block
Delancey Place
1853–80
Private residences

Delancey Place, one of the earliest of the new developments west of Broad Street created by speculative developers, was opened as a street in 1853 on a parcel of land granted by Christ Church. Most of the houses on the north side were completed by 1860, with the remainder finished by 1880. The houses were designed in the Italianate style, but later additions to several houses by Wilson Eyre and Cope and Stewardson have given the block a more Victorian appearance.

Walk down Delancey Place to 19th Street then turn right and return to Spruce Street. Turn left on **(3) Spruce Street** to 22nd Street.

2000 and 2100 Blocks Spruce Street
1868–80
Private residences

18

The 2000 and 2100 blocks of Spruce Street are representative of the outstanding Victorian row houses throughout the entire Rittenhouse Square area.

Brownstone became a popular building material in the 19th century because it was cheap, attractive and easily carved. Many brownstone houses were built prior to 1880, when it was discovered that the stone did not wear well over time. The brownstones on these two blocks are fine examples of the many found in the Rittenhouse Square are. They show the influence of the Second Empire style in the use of mansard roofs and round-headed windows with keystones and framing pilasters.

At the corner of 21st and Spruce streets are four of the finest Victorian row houses in the city. The three brick houses were designed by George Hewitt, of which 2100 Spruce, built in 1883 for Lucien Moss, is the most interesting.

In addition to brownstones, the 2100 block has several houses by prominent architects. The house at 2111–13 was designed by Frank Furness. Wilson Eyre designed 2123–25, an elegant Colonial Revival house. The unusual double house at 2132–34, attributed to Furness, is notable for its giant brownstone arch and pressed metal ornament. A colorful note is added to the block by the facade of 2129, which was resurfaced with Mercer tile in 1913.

Before continuing on the tour, take a left on 22nd Street to the **(d) Neill and Mauren Houses** (1890), 315–17 South 22nd Street. These houses show Wilson Eyre's ability to combine different architectural motifs, in this case colonial and medieval. Note the finely crafted doors, which are well-preserved examples of Arts and Crafts wood construction, and the huge gambrel roof which makes the two houses look like one.

Return to Spruce Street and walk back to 21st Street. Turn left on to 21st Street and proceed past Walnut to the **(4) Thomas Hockley House** (1875/1894), 235 South 21st Street.

Thomas Hockley House
1875/1894
Frank Furness
Private residence

Thomas Hockley, an influential lawyer, was an early supporter of Frank Furness. He assisted Furness in obtaining commissions for a number of his later buildings. Furness designed this house when he was just emerging as a leading architect.

The house has the standard Victorian forms, such as the mansard roof, pointed dormers and projecting bay windows. But the ornament and the variety of brick patterns is distinctively Furness. There are variations of cut, pressed, diapered and diagonally laid brick; string-courses and stepped corbels; and a blunt headed chimney, which seems to grow out of the wall from corbeled stems. The oversized, formalized flower designs in the porch tympanums resemble Furness's use of similar motifs on the facade of the Pennsylvania Academy. The use of brickwork to create rich textures and patterns was copied in many other houses of the period.

Continue north along 21st Street to Walnut Street. At the corner is the **(e) Second Presbyterian Church** (1869–72), 2036 Walnut Street, designed by Henry Sims with a tower and chapel added by Frank Furness in 1900. *Turn right on Walnut Street and walk back to Rittenhouse Square.* At the corner of Walnut and 19th streets is **(f) the Church of the Holy Trinity** (1856–59), by John Notman. The church is one of the first accurate renditions of the Romanesque style in the country. The interior is relatively simple, in keeping with the simple service of the Low Church, but it has beautiful stencil work on the vaulted ceiling.

The tour ends where it began in Rittenhouse Square.

City Hall Tour

Center Square was one of the five squares set aside for public use in William Penn's original plan for Philadelphia. When the decision was made to locate the new City Hall on Center Square in 1870, the surrounding area became the focus of commercial development. At the time, Center Square was on the edge of the developed area of the city. There were several civic institutions along Broad Street and a few houses built by prominent citizens. All that changed as department stores, office buildings and banks surrounded City Hall. The importance of the area was strengthened when the Pennsylvania and Reading railroads located their stations west and east of City Hall.

In the past few decades, the railroad stations have provided the focus for even greater commercial and retail growth. During the 1950s, the Pennsylvania Railroad's Broad Street Station was demolished to create the Penn Center office complex. Retail development remained east of City Hall, where a new shopping mall, the Gallery, has been constructed adjacent to the Reading Terminal. More recently, the City Hall area has been transformed by some of the city's largest construction projects, including the Pennsylvania Convention Center and four tall office buildings, all of which exceed the traditional height limit of the City Hall Tower.

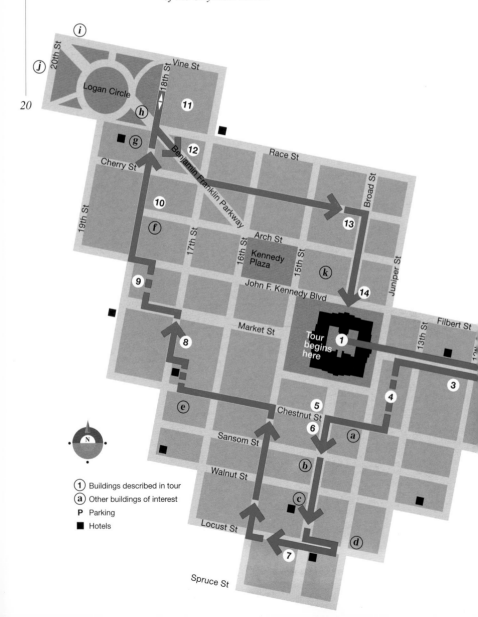

The tour begins at City Hall and then proceeds through the older portions of the area along Market and Broad streets. The tour returns to City Hall after passing through the office sector to the west and along the beautiful Benjamin Franklin Parkway.

The first building on the tour is **(1) City Hall** (1871–1901), Broad and Market streets.

City Hall is the largest municipal building in the country and the finest example of the Second Empire style. It contains 14 $1/_2$ acres of floor space, occupied by city and county offices, courtrooms and several ornately detailed public spaces.

The building is organized around a central public courtyard which is reached through monumental arched portals on all four sides. Second Empire motifs are combined with an abundance of sculpture to give the exterior a rich yet intimately scaled appearance. Solid granite, 22 feet thick in some portions, forms the first floor and supports a brick structure faced with white marble.

City Hall
1871–1901
John McArthur, Jr.,
architect, with
Thomas U. Walter
Open to the public

Alexander Milne Calder created all the sculpture on the building. Calder also designed the 27-ton cast-iron statue of William Penn atop the tower, which is the largest single piece of sculpture on any building in the world. The 548-foot high tower is the world's tallest masonry structure without a steel frame. It is granite up to the clock, then cast iron painted to look like stone.

Public spaces within the building are among the most lavish in the city. The City Council chamber is ornately detailed and uses such expensive materials as alabaster on the walls. The Mayor's Reception Room is extremely handsome; it has a blue and gold ceiling, beautiful woodwork and red Egyptian marble columns. Conversation Hall, restored to its original elegance in 1982 by Day and Zimmermann Associates, is dominated by a magnificent chandelier. John Ord, chief architect from 1890–94, is thought to have ben responsible for much of the interior detailing. The tower is open to the public and affords a wonderful view of the city.

Leave City Hall by the east portico and walk along Market Street to 12th Street to the **(2) Reading Terminal** (1891–93) and Pennsylvania Convention Center (1993–94).

When steam locomotives eliminated the fear of fire from wood-burning engines, the Reading Railroad built a inner-city terminal on the site occupied by the Franklin Farmers' Market since 1860. The market, now known as the Reading Terminal Market, was given space under the train shed where it remains to this day.

The Head House on Market Street originally contained waiting rooms and offices. It is constructed of wrought- and cast-iron columns, wrought-iron and steel beams and brick floors. The structural system was designed by the Wilson Brothers, as was the train shed, but the Italian Renaissance exterior of the Head House was applied over the structural system by a consulting architect, Frank Kimball of New York.

Reading Terminal
1891–93
The Wilson Brothers
Open to the public

The train shed is the only surviving single-span arched train shed in the country. It was the largest single-span structure

21

in the world when completed. The shed has been preserved by incorporating it into the Pennsylvania Convention Center. A Grand Hall, Ballroom and meeting rooms are located in the shed which is connected to a new building to the north containing 440,000 square feet of exhibit space. The Convention Center and train shed renovations were designed by the architectural team of Thompson, Ventulett, Stainback Associates; the Vitetta Group; Kelly/Maiello Architects; and Livingston Rosenwinkel P.C.

Walk up 12th Street and go into the Reading Terminal Farmers' Market and then return to Market Street to the **(3) PSFS Building** (1930–32), 12 South 12th Street, one of the most important buildings in the city.

When the Philadelphia Savings Fund Society decided to build a new headquarters, the directors chose a site near the Reading Terminal and Wanamaker's department store, where they already had a successful branch bank. George Howe was retained as architect. Howe had a national reputation for his pastoral suburban houses but recently had become an advocate of the International style emerging in Europe. PSFS marked Howe's break with his past. He left his former architectural partners, Mellor and Meigs, and entered into partnership with William Lescaze, a Swiss architect. Together they designed the first International style skyscraper in the country.

PSFS is a masterpiece; it is the finest 20th-century building in the city and one of the most important examples of the International Style in the country. The exterior form is a sophisticated expression of the different functions within the building. The base contains a retail store on the first floor, with the banking room located above. Bank offices above are set back from the facade of the office tower, which rises to a complicated roof structure and a prominent sign. At the rear of the building elevator shafts and service elements form a separate unit. To emphasize further the contrasting elements of the design, different material and colors were used. Highly polished gray granite covers the base; sand-colored limestone is used for the facade of the bank offices. The office tower has exposed vertical columns covered with the same limestone and gray brick spandrels. The huge rear wall of the service core is made of glazed and unglazed black brick. Even though PSFS was built at the height of the Depression, expensive materials and furnishings were used throughout. The stainless steel hardware and most of the furniture were custom-designed by the architects, as there was no inventory of modern fixtures in the United States. The most dramatic interior space is the high-ceilinged banking room. Subdued colors; polished materials like marble, glass and stainless steel; and gently curved balconies give the room an exceptional quality.

After visiting the banking room, walk west along Market Street, past 13th Street and enter the **(4) John Wanamaker Department Store** (1902–11).

John Wanamaker began selling ready-made clothing in 1861. By the time he moved his store to 13th and Market streets, it had become a full-fledged department store, one of the first in the country.

22

PSFS Building
1930–32
Howe and Lescaze

John Wanamaker Department Store
1902–11
D.H. Burnham and Company, with John T. Windrim
Renovated 1991, Ewing Cole Cherry Brott
Open to the public

When Wanamaker decided to construct a new store he retained Daniel Burnham, the great Chicago architect, who collaborated with John T. Windrim. Wanamaker wanted to rebuild on the same site, but he also wanted the existing store to remain in operation. As result, the building was constructed in three stages, which required considerable care to make sure that the joining of the stages was invisible. As the first phase of construction was completed, the settlement of the building was measured and used to determine the design for the next addition.

The exterior has little ornament or detail; it is a simple block, organized in three horizontal divisions. The handsome granite and limestone facade is an adaptation of the Renaissance palace, greatly enlarged in scale. Inside, the selling floors were organized around a spectacular central court that rises five floors. It is the most impressive interior space in any commercial building in the city.

After walking through the Grand Court at Wanamaker's exit on the Chestnut Street side, turn right and walk to Broad Street. Note the **(a) Keystone National Bank** (1887/1890), 1326 Chestnut Street, a flamboyant design by Willis Hale derived from French chateaux of the Loire Valley. At the northwest corner of Broad and Chestnut streets is the **(5) Girard Trust Company** (1905–08), 34–36 South Broad Street.

The Girard Trust building is the city's best example of this neoclassical style introduced in the United States at the 1893 Columbian Exposition in Chicago. Frank Furness originally attempted to design the bank in his heavy Victorian manner. The bank resisted, however, and the final design is a combination of Furness's plans with detailing by Stanford White of McKim, Mead and White, whose firm was responsible for much of the work at the Chicago Exposition.

23

Girard Trust Company
1905–08
McKim, Mead and White
Open to the public

The Girard Trust building is a small jewel surrounded by tall skyscrapers. With its gleaming white marble walls, handsome portico and distinctive dome, it has all the characteristics of a classical temple. Typically, however, the building used modern construction techniques, and behind the marble exterior is a steel-frame structure. The expansive dome, with skylit oculus in the center, is constructed of marble tiles using the techniques developed by Rafael Gustavino. The adjacent office building, also in white marble, was added in 1923 by McKim, Mead and White.

Opposite the bank is the **(6) Land Title Building** (1897), Broad and Chestnut streets.

The Land Title Building is the finest example of early skyscraper design in Philadelphia and the earliest east-coast example of this style by a major Chicago architect. The sixteen-story structure, faced in buff brick, is divided into three parts. The two-story base, faced with granite, is unified by a rusticated Ionic arcade. The central portion of the building has alternating strips of projecting and flat windows, typical of the Chicago Commercial style. The continuous vertical piers, terminating in arches at the top, express the frame and were standard devices used to emphasize the building's height. The top is treated as a separate unit,

Land Title Building
1897
D.H. Burnham and Company

with a prominent overhanging roof and elaborate cornice.

Although built as a speculative office building, the interiors were finished in expensive materials, including marble and hardwood floors and marble wainscoting in the corridors.

From Chestnut Street walk south on Broad Street to Locust Street. Along the way are several distinctive buildings. The **(b) Union League** (1864–65), 140 South Broad Street, designed by John Fraser, was one of the many political clubs organized during the Civil War years. Its brick and brownstone building, an early example of the Second Empire style, was one of the few buildings erected in Philadelphia during the Civil War. Further down Broad Street past Walnut Street is the **(c) Bellevue Stratford Hotel** (1902–13), once the city's most fashionable hotel. It was designed by G.W. and W.D. Hewitt, two of the most prolific Philadelphia architects of the 19th century. The hotel closed after an outbreak of Legionnaires disease in 1976, but reopened again after being remodeled in 1980 and 1989 by Day and Zimmermann Associates, now the Vitetta Group.

Academy of Music
1855–57
Napoleon LeBrun and
Gustave Runge

The **(7) Academy of Music** (1855–57), 232–46 South Broad Street, marks the start of Philadelphia's cultural district, known as the Avenue of the Arts. This area contains a number of important performing arts institutions including the University of the Arts.

Philadelphia's musical development was slow compared with other cities, partly because of the dominant Quaker conservatism. Musical entertainment was provided in small theaters and concert halls but by the 1850s the public was eager for opera on a grand sale. A site for a concert hall was acquired on Broad Street, a largely undeveloped, quiet location.

The plan, selected by a competition, was modeled after La Scala in Milan. LeBrun and Runge fashioned the interior like a huge barrel, excavating a well beneath the parquet, ballooning out the ceiling in a dome, placing a sounding board in the orchestra pit and curving the rear walls of the auditorium. For all the walls to settle, the building stood for a year without a roof. When finished the academy was acoustically unsurpassed.

The neo-Baroque interior is one of the most lavish in the city. Huge Corinthian columns mark the proscenium and an immense Victorian chandelier hangs from a ceiling decorated with murals by Karl Heinrich Schmolze. The Academy is the oldest musical auditorium in the country still serving its original purpose.

Before turning west on Locust Street to continue the tour, take a brief detour to Juniper and Locust streets to see the **(d) Clarence Moore House** (1890), 1321 Locust Street, a very distinctive and imaginatively designed house by Wilson Eyre. The exterior is a rich study in contrasting textures and styles, including Gothic arched windows, a Venetian loggia and a tower derived from French chateaux. *Then return along Locust Street to 15th Street, turn right and walk north to Chestnut Street. At Chestnut Street turn left and walk to the 1600 block.* On the south side of the street is the **(e) WCAU Building** (1928), 1620 Chestnut Street, designed by Harry Sternfeld and Gabriel Roth and renovated in 1983 by Kopple, Sheward and Day. It is one of the finest examples of Art Deco design in Philadelphia.

On the north side of the street is **(8) Liberty Place** (1987–90).

Liberty Place has three components: One Liberty Place

(1987), 1650 Market Street, the tallest building in the city and the first to break the height limit of the City Hall tower; Two Liberty Place (1990), 50 South 16th Street, and the Shops at Liberty Place with the Ritz-Carlton Hotel (1990).

When new office buildings were developed west of City Hall in the 1950s, an informal gentleman's agreement limited their height to no greater than the 491-foot height of City Hall Tower, thereby enabling the statue of William Penn atop the tower to preside symbolically over the city. Willard Rouse's proposal to build a higher office building sparked controversy and extensive public debate.

One Liberty Place, at a height of 960 feet to the top of its spire, is the tallest building in the city and the most prominent landmark day or night. The 61-story tower is set on a three-story podium which is sheathed in blue-gray polished granite interrupted by bay windows for retail uses. The tower has a silver-blue aluminum grid which holds horizontal bands of blue glass and gray granite at the corners. The central portion of the facade is silver metallic glass, interrupted by bands of gray granite at every fourth floor, giving scale and decoration to the facade. This combination of silver and blue glass gives the building a shimmering quality and delicacy in spite of its massive size. The top of the building, sheathed entirely in glass, is formed by the repetitive use of a gable form, resulting in a silhouette reminiscent of the Chrysler Building. Linear bands of light along the gable edges give the building a striking presence on the skyline at night.

25

Liberty Place
1987–90
Murphy/Jahn and the
Zeidler Roberts
Partnership

Mellon Center
1990
Kohn Pederson Fox

Bell Atlantic Tower
1991
The Kling-Lindquist
Partnership

Two Liberty Place, uses the same architectural vocabulary but in a more subdued fashion. It also has a three-story podium sheathed in the same blue-gray polished granite, with generous windows, in this case for the office lobby. The facade continues the pattern of bands of masonry and blue tinted glass at the corner, but uses darker masonry, and silver metallic glass in the center. A single gable roof, also illuminated on its edges, crowns the tower.

One and Two Liberty Place are connected by an elegant two-story arcade of retail stores. Corner entrances lead to a glass enclosed rotunda surrounded by two levels of shops and a large food court.

Liberty Place is an outstanding achievement of both urban design and architecture. Its dramatic break with the past, carried out at such a high standard of excellence, offered Philadelphia a symbol of new possibilities and civic pride.

Turn left on Market Street at 17th Street. On the north side of Market Street is the **(9) Mellon Center** (1990), 1735 Market Street.

Mellon Center's large site allows the 53-story office tower to take the form of a gigantic, free standing obelisk on axis with City Hall. The five-story base is sheathed in granite, with modestly articulated ornamentation. The tapering tower has central bays of vertical columns, expressing the structural system. A lattice, pyramidal structure, housing the building's cooling system, tops the tower and completes the obelisk analogy. A public winter garden for exhibits and displays is housed in a small glass structure between the tower and an older office building.

Walk through Mellon Center's elegant lobbies of polished marble to John F. Kennedy Boulevard then turn left to 18th Street and walk north to Arch Street. The **(f) Arch Street Presbyterian Church** (1853–55), 1724 Arch Street, Joseph C. Hoxie, has a copper dome influenced by the design for St. Paul's Cathedral in London. The sanctuary is a masterpiece of the Classical Revival style and one of the most beautiful interiors in the city.

Directly across the street is the **(10) Bell Atlantic Tower** (1991), 1750 Arch Street.

The Bell Atlantic Tower is a contrast to its predecessors in almost every way. Because the site is bisected by the zone of special design controls along the Benjamin Franklin Parkway which limit the height of buildings, the office tower was placed on the southern edge of the site and designed with stepped-back corners to avoid the line of controls.

The tower consists of a series of slabs corresponding in width to the set-backs in plan, ending in a flat roof. Warm red granite accented by honed granite spandrels up the center of the broad facades and by polished granite around the entrance porticos, gives the building a more sedate and dignified character than One Liberty Place or Mellon Center. At night, the stepped-slabs are illuminated at the top of the building giving the appearance of a cascade of light.

Although the tower lacks the dramatic impact of its predecessors, the choice of materials and simplicity of form give the building a refined grace and elegance on the Philadelphia skyline.

From the Bell Atlantic Tower walk north along 18th Street to the Benjamin Franklin Parkway passing the **(g) Four Seasons Hotel and One Logan Square** (1982–83), Kohn Pederson Fox, an elegant building complex and one of the first in the city designed in the post-Modern style. The **(h) Benjamin Franklin Parkway** is one of the outstanding examples of Beaux Arts urban design in the country. It was carved out of the existing fabric of the city in 1917, creating a diagonal connection from City Hall through Logan Circle to Faire Mount, formerly the site of a reservoir serving the city and now the location of the Philadelphia Museum of Art (see page 31). The Parkway was designed by the landscape architect Jacques Greber and modeled after the Champs Elysées in Paris. The buildings around Logan Circle are modeled after the twin palaces on the Place de la Concorde which occupied a similar position on the boulevard. The **(i) Free Library** (1917–27), 1900 Vine Street, was designed by Horace Trumbauer, but probably heavily influenced by Julian Abele, a black architect who was Trumbauer's chief designer and had made recent trips to Paris.

On the far side of Logan Circle is the **(j) Franklin Institute**. The original building, designed by John T. Windram in 1930, contains a central rotunda with a huge marble statue of

Benjamin Franklin. The Institute's Mandell Futures Center (1990), Geddes Brecher Qualls Cunningham, contains interactive computer exhibits and an Imax theater.

Just north of the Parkway on 18th Street is the **(11) Cathedral of SS. Peter and Paul** (1846–64).

Although Catholics had always been present in the city, their numbers were not significant until after the Irish immigration in the 1830s. By 1844, the Irish population was large enough to support the building of a cathedral. The cathedral is the oldest building on Logan Circle. It was one of the most sumptuous churches in the country when completed. The interior is designed in a grand Italian Renaissance style. Notable features include the domed baldachino over the altar, the giant Corinthian pilasters encircling the nave and transept and the deeply coffered barrel vault over the nave. Norman and Reverend John T. Mahoney added the dome and the elegant brownstone facade after 1850.

Cathedral of SS. Peter and Paul
1846–64
Napoleon LeBrun and John Notman
Open to the public

Return to the Parkway and walk towards City Hall, passing the **(12) United Fund Building** (1969), between 17th and 18th streets.

27

The design controls for the Parkway are intended to ensure that buildings east of 18th street create a narrow urban space. The United Fund Building is responsive to the intent of the parkway controls and its urban context.

The small, seven-story structure conforms to its trapezoidal site. Each elevation responds to the unique conditions of its orientation. The north side

United Fund Building
1969
Mitchell/Giurgola Associates

is a curtain wall of gray-tinted glass, which allows maximum light for the office floors. The west wall is shielded from the sun by horizontal concrete sunscreens. The south wall, of structural concrete, has deeply recessed windows that block the south sunlight but afford views of Logan Circle.

At 17th and the Parkway turn left on Cherry Street and continue for three blocks to Broad Street. At the corner of Broad and Cherry streets is the **(13) Pennsylvania Academy of Fine Arts** (1872–76).

The academy, founded in 1805, was the first art school and museum in the country. Its most famous student was Thomas Eakins, who became a dominating presence as a teacher from 1876–86. The academy is the most outstanding example of Frank Furness's work and one of the most magnificent Victorian buildings in the country. In con-

Pennsylvania Academy of the Fine Arts
1872–76
Furness and Hewitt
Open to the public

28

trast to the somber tones of previous Victorian architecture, the interior is an explosion of color: the walls have gilt floral patterns incised on a field of Venetian red; the cerulean blue ceiling is sprinkled with silver stars; the gallery walls are plum, ochre, sand and olive green.

Furness's work is characterized by overscaled and unusually proportioned structural details and the extensive use of carved floral patterns. These can be seen throughout the interior in the form of cast-bronze foliation along the stair rail, compression in columns in the galleries and the use of dwarf columns supporting massive arches.

The facade is an amalgam of historical styles, fused in an aggressively personal manner. The pointed arches, floral ornament and use of color are derived from English Gothic design, while the mansard roof, projecting central pavilion and panels of incised tryglyphs come from French sources. This riot of forms is executed in rusticated brownstone, dressed sandstone and polished pink granite, red pressed brick and purplish terra-cotta.

For many decades the academy was considered to be an unattractive building and its ornamental brilliance was obscured. A comprehensive restoration in 1976 by Day and Zimmermann Associates returned the building to its original, and extraordinary, appearance.

From the academy walk south on Broad Street toward City Hall. On the west side of Broad Street is the **(k) Municipal Services Building** (1960), Vincent G. Kling and Associates. On the east side is the **(14) Masonic Temple** (1868–73/1890s), 1 North Broad Street.

Masonic Temple
1868–73/1890s
James Windrim and George Herzog
Open to the public

Freemasonry prospered in Philadelphia from colonial times. Several temples were built, culminating in this magnificent structure, one of the world's greatest Masonic temples.

The Masons held a competition and selected Brother James Windrim, a 27-year-old freemason, as the winner. Windrim's design was modeled on a medieval style known as Norman. This is reflected in the massive carved doorway that projects from the wall; the aslar stone work; the fortress like towers; and the corbel tables, a round-arch decorated cornice under the roofline.

The temple took five years to build. The interior design was begun 14 years later and took 15 more years to complete. George Herzog, who had trained in the royal workshops of Ludwig I of Munich, was the primary designer. The spectacular interior spaces include seven lodge halls, each lavishly decorated in a specific style. The most renowned is the Egyptian Hall, replete with accurate hieroglyphics. The temple was one of the first buildings in the city to be lighted by electricity.

The tour concludes at City Hall.

Buildings Not on Walking Tours

In addition to the buildings on the four walking tours, there are other outstanding buildings in Center City and immediately adjacent to Center City that are easy to reach by public transportation and well worth the short trip. These are listed below, with brief descriptions and photographs. In addition, there is one building located about a forty minute drive from Center City that is of special significance. This is the Beth Shalom Synagogue, the only major building by Frank Lloyd Wright in the Philadelphia area. A description of the building and directions to reach it are included at the end of this list.

Buildings in Center City

Pennsylvania Hospital, 1755–94/1805
8th and Pine streets
Samuel Rhoads/David Evans, Jr.
Center Pavilion Restored 1977
Bartley Long Mirenda Architects

Pennsylvania Hospital, the first hospital in the colonies, was built on a site far from the noises and smells of the city. The center section is one of the finest examples of the Federal style in the country. The facade shows a new sophistication in public architecture. Monochromatic brick replaces the checkerboard pattern of Flemish bond and glazed headers. The first floor is faced with marble, and giant Corinthian marble pilasters stretch from the second floor to the cornice. The center pavilion projects slightly and has a fashionable oval window in its pediment. Evans designed a circular amphitheater on the top floor, marked by an exterior balustrade. It was here that modern surgery was first performed in the United States.

Portico Row, 1831–32
900–930 Spruce Street
Thomas U. Walter
Private residences

Portico Row was built by real estate speculator John Savage, who hired Walter to design sixteen houses for sale to upper-middle-class lawyers, doctors and merchants. The houses were elaborately designed on both exterior and interior. The brick facades, with marble lintels, are distinguished by a series of projecting porticos supported by marble Ionic columns. Each portico provides entrance to two houses. The interior rooms were spacious and richly finished. Highly-polished marble was used for all fireplaces, walnut or mahogany for doors and trim. Even water closets were built of walnut, and the bathroom floors were marble.

The Atrium, 1982
Market Street between 19th and 20th streets
Cope Linder Associates
Open to the public

In contrast to typical tall office buildings, The Atrium creates a prestigious office setting by constructing a low, eight-story structure around a skylit atrium extending the full height of the building. This atrium is designed as a gigantic interior greenhouse. Hanging plants on the end walls complement the lush tropical landscape of the main floor. The predominantly glass walls facing the atrium have balconies and small terraces projecting into space. Terraced, landscaped courts step down to the lower-level offices of the Philadelphia Stock Exchange, the building's principal tenant. Large windows allow visitors to watch the activities on the exchange floor.

30

4

Commerce Square, 1987, 1992
Market Street between 20th and 21st streets
Pei Cobb Freed and Partners

Commerce Square created a civic setting as well as office center in an area with few surrounding amenities. The heart of the project is a handsome landscaped public plaza designed by Hanna-Olin Ltd. The plaza contains a circular fountain surrounded by tree-shaded outdoor cafes and retail shops. The granite paving, inset with red pavers and black squares, extends the materials and patterns of the towers.

The twin 40-story office towers are set back in a series of slabs to reduce their scale and allow natural light to reach the courtyard most of the day. Each slab is topped by a parapet with geometric openings lightening the edge of the building at the skyline. The 45-foot height line of the lower slab and ground floor arcade create a pedestrian scale. Horizontal bans of gray glass and gray Caledonia granite inset with squares of darker granite also help to reduce the scale, except along the short sides of the towers where paired square windows form a vertical seam emphasizing the height.

Parkway House, 1952–53
22nd Street and Pennsylvania Avenue
Gabriel Roth and Elizabeth Fleischer
Private residences

31

5

Parkway House was one of the first postwar luxury apartment buildings in the city. It is an exceptionally fine design, with elements from both the Art Deco and International styles. The form of the building is derived from a remarkable response to the shape and location of the site. Two side wings of the U-shaped plan step down toward the parkway, creating generous terraces for many of the apartments. Other apartments have curved-glass projecting window bays, which are organized in vertical rows on the main facade. These elements create the only decoration on an otherwise plain brick structure and are more characteristic of buildings of the 1930s than the 1950s, reflecting Roth's Art Deco background. The building is also noteworthy because it was one of the first in the city designed by a woman architect.

Philadelphia Museum of Art, 1916–28
Benjamin Franklin Parkway and 26th Street
Horace Trumbauer, C. Clark Zantzinger, Charles L. Borie, Jr.
Open to the public

After many years of discussion, a site for a new museum was selected on the hill known as Faire Mount, at the end of the Benjamin Franklin Parkway. Trumbauer's chief designer, Julian Abele, the first black graduate of the University of Pennsylvania architecture school, returned from Greece with the idea of building three temples on a solid rock base. The final design is a compromise among his ideas and those of the other architects.

6

The museum is reached from the parkway by the monumental flight of stairs flanked by cascading fountains. The stairs lead to a large terrace with a spectacular view of the city. The museum consists of three interconnected temple structures with very tall porticos, topped by finely detailed pediments.

The pediment of the north temple contains a brilliantly colored terra-cotta sculpture with 13 figures, representing sacred and profane love. The warm, yellow ashlar on the facade and gabled blue tile roof give the building a distinctive appearance.

In addition to its outstanding art collection, the museum contains a number of rooms representing different architectural periods, most of which were built as WPA projects during the 1930s. They include a medieval cloister, a Japanese teahouse, a Chinese temple, an Indian temple, a French Empire room and many others.

Buildings Outside Center City

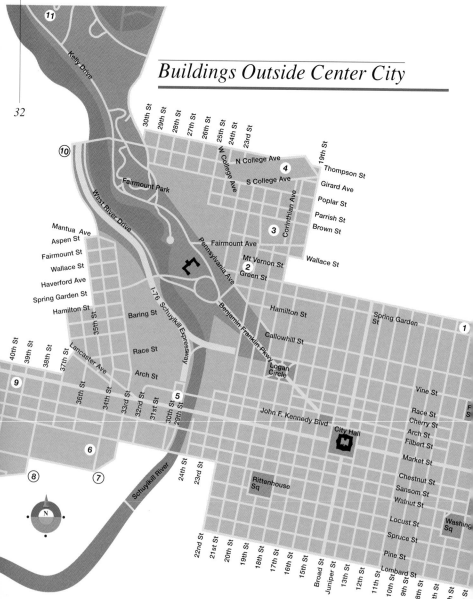

Guild House, 1960–63
7th and Spring Garden Streets
Venturi and Rauch with Cope and Lippincott
Private residences

1

Guild House, an apartment building for low-income elderly persons, is an outstanding example of the ability to create a distinctive building from ordinary materials and forms.

The building is dominated by a six-story entrance facade designed in the classical tradition. The first-floor base is faced in white glazed brick; the upper floors have balconies puncturing the flat facade and the top floor terminates the composition with the flat arch of the common room window. From the facade, the building steps back on either side, permitting most apartments an east, west or south exposure onto small landscaped areas.

The composition of the elevation is particularly skillful in the placement, size and shape of standard metal windows. By contrast with the articulated form and varied windows of the front elevation, the rear of the building is a flat surface with uniform windows, in keeping with the ordinary character of the surrounding housing. On the interior, apartments are arranged along a corridor that bends and turns, giving a more intimate scale and informal organization.

33

Kemble-Bergdol House, 1890
2201–05 Green Street
James Windrim with George Herzog
Private residence

2

William H. Kemble, a financier, built an elaborate mansion, which he later sold to the Bergdol family, owners of one of the city's largest breweries.

The house is one of the city's finest examples of Italianate brownstone design, a style whose rich and elaborate carving appealed to late 19th-century industrialists. The symmetrical facade is very imposing and has a generous portico entrance. Porches on the rear and west elevations are constructed of copper, iron and glass. The lavish interior was principally the work of Herzog, interior designer of the Masonic Temple. It has richly carved woodwork and plaster walls, hand-stenciled with designs in gold leaf.

(After seeing the Kemble-Bergdol House take a walk down Green Street to 15th Street. Green Street was developed from 1860 to 1890 when speculative builders followed wealthy industrialists into the area and created quality row houses for the rising managerial middle class. The most notable houses are 2223, designed by Willis Hale, which has an unusual facade of brick enlivened by multicolored ceramic tile; 2220, a Romanesque revival house with a corner tower; and 2301 Green. The handsome brownstones at 2144–46, with a decorative ribbon carved in stone over the doorway, are attributed to Wilson Eyre. The brownstones at 1901–03 have been attributed to The Wilson Brothers. The distinctive, exuberant Queen Anne style house at 1533 has been attributed to John Fraser.)

Eastern State Penitentiary, 1823–36
Fairmount Avenue at 21st Street
John Haviland
Open to the public

Early Quakers believed that criminals could be reformed by placing them in solitary confinement to contemplate their past deeds and seek divine guidance. Eastern State was based on this philosophy. The original plan consisted of seven long cell blocks radiating from a central surveillance rotunda. Each cell block contained individual solitary cells and work yards. The cell blocks and prison yard were enclosed behind a massive stone wall with such Gothic details as lancet windows, square towers flanking the entrance and battlemented turrets at the corners. The design was enormously influential and copied by more than 500 prisons around the world.

Up to its closing in 1972, buildings were steadily added, obscuring the original plan. Some famous prisoners stayed here including the bank robber Willie Sutton. Since 1972, the prison has been in a state of deterioration and only recently opened to the public. It presents a rare opportunity to see the inside of prison life from jail cells and work areas to the guards' central observation tower.

Founder's Hall, Girard College, 1833–47
Girard and Corinthian Avenues
Thomas U. Walter
Open to the public by appointment

In his will, Stephen Girard, the first American multimillionaire, bequeathed $2 million for a school for "poor white male orphans."

Walter's winning design in the architectural competition was changed by Nicholas Biddle, president of the board of trustees, who wanted to build the most correct Greek temple in America. In response to this direction, Walter wrapped marble Corinthian columns around the entire building and raised the temple on flight of steps. The roof and walls are covered with local Chester County marble. Inside, the four rooms to a floor, required by Girard's will, are vaulted. Under the roof, pendentive domes with skylights make use of the space behind the entablature.

Founder's Hall, one of the most expensive buildings of its time, was the climax of the Greek Revival style in America. The building worked poorly and was abandoned as a schoolhouse in 1916. It remains a tribute to Stephen Girard, whose tomb is on the first floor. Girard College was integrated in 1968 following years of significant civil rights litigation.

30th Street Station, 1929–34
30th Street and JFK Boulevard
Graham, Anderson, Probst and White
Restored 1991, Dan Peter Kopple and Associates
Open to the public

5

Only a few railroad stations as grand as 30th Street Station remain in the country today. Like others of the time, it has an enormous interior waiting room. This room is faced with marble and covered with a coffered ceiling painted in red, gold and cream. Natural light enters through glass walls at both ends, which contain catwalks connecting the flanking wings of the building.

The exterior has monumental, columned porte cochères on the east and west facades. Although classical elements are used on the facade, their simple form indicates a compromise between historical and emerging modern styles.

Anne and Jerome Fisher Fine Arts Library, 1888–90
34th and Walnut streets
Frank Furness; Restored 1990, Venturi, Scott Brown and Associates, with the Clio Group and Marianna Thomas, Architect
Open to the public

6

35

The library is one of the finest remaining examples of the work of Frank Furness. When completed it was the most innovative library building in the country. It was one of the first to separate reading room from book stacks. The most impressive interior spaces are the catalog room and the reading room. The catalog room is dominated by a monumental fireplace. The reading room is surrounded by study alcoves and lit from windows above. Curved iron beams radiate from the center of the ceiling to delicate terracotta leaves on top of the brick pilasters.

Like most of Furness's buildings, the exterior was highly controversial. It contains a rich use of brick and stone with terra-cotta panels, short heavy columns and unusual details, such as the scalloped crenelations on the tower and gargoyles on the north end.

University Museum, 1893–1926/1969–71
3320 South Street
Wilson Eyre, Frank Miles Day and brother, Cope and Stewardson; Mitchell/Giurgola Associates
Open to the public

The museum is a brilliant example of the 19th-century electric tradition: many historical architectural styles are combined in a unified and original composition. A Japanese gate forms the entrance to an intimately scaled courtyard, created by the main building and wings of the museum. A prominent rotunda dominates the otherwise horizontal tile-covered roofs of main building. White and colored marble, colored brick and varying brick patterns enrich the wall surface; the eaves of the main building are decorated with mosaics.

The interior of the building contains galleries for the museum's outstanding collection of archaeological finds from Egypt, Mesopotamia, Mesoamerica, Asia and other parts of the world. The rotunda, an enormous single room, is lit by arched clerestory windows and covered by a dome surfaced with Mercer tiles. Because the museum was never completed, interior circulation was awkward until the addition of a new wing. The new wing blends with the red brick and tile-roofed exterior of the original building, but on the interior, glass and reinforced concrete are clearly expressed in a successful juxtaposition of old and new styles.

Richards Medical Research Laboratory, 1957–61
37th Street and Hamilton Walk
Louis I. Kahn

The Richards Medical Research Laboratory is considered one of the most significant buildings in modern American architecture. It was the pivotal project in the career of Louis Kahn and transformed him from an influential theoretical architect to one of international importance.

At the Richards Laboratory, Kahn brought together in a unified design several concepts developed previously in other projects. He divided the building into served and servant spaces, giving each its own form and expression. The core tower of the building is poured-in-place concrete; it contains such services as elevators, animal quarters and utilities. The laboratories are located in three eight-story towers, connected to the core. Each of these towers in turn is served by smaller brick shafts containing additional services. The laboratories are open spaces made possible by placing both services and the structural system on the periphery of the building. Within the laboratories, the interlocking grid of supporting precast beams is exposed to allow for easy connection of utility systems to the surrounding towers.

Kahn felt that a building should reflect the way it was built. The innovative precast and poured-in-place concrete system, designed by August E. Komandant, articulates the structural principles of the cantilevered construction while providing visual interest to the facade.

University City Family Housing, 1982–83
Market Street between 39th and 40th streets
Friday Architects
Private residences

This imaginatively designed low income housing complex creates a sense of place for its residents to overcome its predominantly institutional and commercial surroundings. Most of the houses are arranged in rows perpendicular to Market Street, with small backyards and common entrance courts, framed by arches and by a long row of houses on the southern edge of the site, giving privacy to the common open space. Brick is used for the facades facing the entrance courts, which also have Queen Anne-style wood porches with decorated gables and bay windows reflecting Victorian motifs from West Philadelphia. On the back the houses are covered in green aluminum siding, symbolizing the garden side of the building.

George D. Widener Memorial Tree House, 1985
The Philadelphia Zoological Gardens
34th Street and Girard Avenue
Venturi, Rauch and Scott Brown
Open to the public

The 42-acre Philadelphia Zoo contains an interesting collection of buildings by some of the city's most distinguished architects. One of its most interesting features is the Children's Zoo where animals are free to be touched and fed. When the Children's Zoo was redesigned in the 1980's the 1876 Antelope House designed by George Hewitt was transformed into a central feature. Six separate environmental settings were created within the Victorian structure, each designed to enable participants to view these environments as their natural inhabitants would. A large cell honeycomb, for example, allows children to experience what it would be like to be a bee. Fiber-glass, rubber, insulation and other artificial materials were used to create life-like trees, vegetation and animal forms of exaggerated size.

The building derives its name from a 24-foot-high, 16-foot-wide artificial ficus tree which projects through the roof of the existing building into an added cupola.

Not just for children, the Tree House is one of the city's most popular interior spaces.

37

Mount Pleasant, 1761
Mount Pleasant Drive, Fairmount Park
Open to the public

Of all the country estates of colonial Philadelphia, Mount Pleasant was the most elegant. It was built by Captain John MacPherson, a Scottish privateer. He drew on Palladian principles of design, building a main house symmetrically flanked by two small buildings. The distinguishing feature of Mount Pleasant is the projecting pavilion with its pediment. Both the east and west sides of the building have Palladian windows. MacPherson contrasted the texture and color of brick in the horizontal belt courses and corner quoins with a warm-colored stucco ruled to look like stone. This provides a pleasing variation on the usual solid brick or stone houses. The interior is equally handsome, with finely carved paneling.

Building in the Region

Beth Sholom Synagogue, 1959–60
Old York and Foxcroft roads
Elkins Park
Frank Lloyd Wright

Beth Sholom Synagogue is the only major building by Frank Lloyd Wright in the Philadelphia area. In the 1930s Wright envisioned a church in the shape of a gigantic glass pyramid. Like many of his other early conceptual projects, this did not become an actual building until late in his career.

The synagogue consists of a temple seating 1,000 persons and a chapel below. The temple has a hexagonal plan with an inwardly sloping floor. It is brilliantly illuminated by the translucent pyramidal roof, from the center of which hangs a colored-glass chandelier trimmed in incandescent lights. It is a spectacular and inspiring religious space. The pyramid structure, supported by a giant steel tripod, has double walls of plastic sheathed in glass. Along the spines of the pyramid are symbols of the menorah.

To reach Beth Sholom by car take the Schuylkill Expressway to the Roosevelt Expressway and get off at the Broad Street exit. Turn left onto Broad Street (PA 611) and go north approximately two and a half miles. Bear right onto Old York Road and continue for another two miles to Foxcroft Road.

Kids Tour

Many of Philadelphia's best buildings are also of interest to children because of their functions or special character. For visitors traveling with children, or residents who would like to introduce their children to outstanding architecture while also having fun, the following buildings described in this book are of particular interest:

Building	Tour or Location
Independence Hall	Old City Tour, *page 6*
Franklin Court	Old City Tour, *page 6*
Masonic Temple	City Hall Tour, *page 20*
City Hall and Tower	City Hall Tour, *page 20*
Reading Terminal	City Hall Tour, *page 20*
John Wanamaker Store	City Hall Tour, *page 20*
Philadelphia Museum of Art	Buildings in Center City, *page 27*
Eastern State Penitentiary	Buildings Outside Center City, *page 30*
University Museum	Buildings Outside Center City, *page 30*
Widener Tree House at Zoo	Buildings Outside Center City, *page 30*

Mandell Futures Center at the Franklin Institute
1990
Geddes Brecher
Qualls Cunningham
Open to the public

Three other architecturally distinctive buildings of interest to children are the Mandell Futures Center at the Franklin Institute (noted on the City Hall tour, *page 20*); the New Jersey State Aquarium on the Camden Waterfront, which can be reached from Penn's Landing via the Riverbus; and Fort Mifflin in South Philadelphia.

Thomas H. Kean New Jersey State Aquarium
1993
The Hillier Group
Open to the public

Fort Mifflin
1772–98/1870s
Thomas Mifflin
and Pierre Charles
L'Enfant
Open to the public

Index